Mealtime for Zoo Animals

by Caroline Arnold   **photographs by Richard Hewett**

Carolrhoda Books, Inc./Minneapolis

What do zoo animals eat?
They eat some of the same
foods you do.
They eat other things, too.

elephant

A monkey uses its strong teeth to bite a piece of fruit.

monkey

A giraffe grabs some hay between its large lips.

giraffe

A rhinoceros is a
giant living lawn mower.

rhinoceros

A young hippopotamus plays while its mother chews hay.

hippopotamuses

A cheetah uses its sharp teeth for tearing meat.

cheetah

A killer whale
swallows fish whole.

killer whale

A flamingo looks
for small plants and
tiny shellfish to eat.

flamingo

17

A young orangutan munches on broccoli.

orangutan

A panda's favorite food is young bamboo.

panda

A peacock tastes a flower.

peacock

A giant tortoise nibbles a leaf.

tortoise

Two tapirs pick up fruit, hay, and dry food with their long snouts.

tapirs

Zoo animals eat many kinds of food.
Food gives all animals energy and helps them grow big and strong.
Food helps you grow, too.

koalas

Where can I find...

zebra

Caroline Arnold has written more than one hundred books for children. Many of the books are about animals. Caroline lives with her husband in Los Angeles, California.

Richard Hewett worked for magazines before he discovered children's books. He, too, has created many books about animals. Richard lives with his wife in Los Angeles, California.

This book is available in two bindings: ISBN 1-57505-286-5 (lib. bdg.) ISBN 1-57505-389-6 (trade bdg.)

Carolrhoda Books, Inc., c/o The Lerner Publishing Group
241 First Avenue North, Minneapolis, MN 55401 U.S.A.

Website address: www.lernerbooks.com

Library of Congress Cataloging-in-Publication Data

Arnold, Caroline.
   Mealtime for zoo animals / by Caroline Arnold ; photographs by Richard Hewett.
       p.   cm.
   Includes index.
   Summary: Photographs and simple text describe the wide variety of foods eaten by animals in the zoo.
   ISBN 1-57505-286-5 (alk. paper)
   1. Zoo animals—Feeding and feeds—Juvenile literature. [1. Zoo animals.
2. Animals—Food habits.] I. Hewett, Richard, ill. II. Title.
QL77.5.A8   1999
636.088'9—dc21   97-43099

Manufactured in the United States of America
1 2 3 4 5 6 – JR – 04 03 02 01 00 99